T0144965

A tale told by
**LYNN BATTAGLIA**

As relayed to her by a Certain Mole Rat

# The
# SPACE
# of Not Knowing

Illustrated by
**ANNE FIZZARD**

Copyright © 2022 Lynn Battaglia.

All rights reserved. No part of this book may be used or reproduced by any means, graphic, electronic, or mechanical, including photocopying, recording, taping or by any information storage retrieval system without the written permission of the author except in the case of brief quotations embodied in critical articles and reviews.

Balboa Press books may be ordered through booksellers or by contacting:

Balboa Press
A Division of Hay House
1663 Liberty Drive
Bloomington, IN 47403
www.balboapress.com
844-682-1282

Because of the dynamic nature of the Internet, any web addresses or links contained in this book may have changed since publication and may no longer be valid. The views expressed in this work are solely those of the author and do not necessarily reflect the views of the publisher, and the publisher hereby disclaims any responsibility for them.

ISBN: 979-8-7652-2613-1 (sc)
ISBN: 979-8-7652-2614-8 (e)

Library of Congress Control Number: 2022904858

Print information available on the last page.

Balboa Press rev. date:  06/06/2022

BALBOA.PRESS
A DIVISION OF HAY HOUSE

A secret space is deep inside of you

That's only known to just a certain few.

This space is very wide and tall and big,

And for those into magic, quite the thing!

"The Space of Not Knowing" is where it's at.

Just follow your guide, the naked mole rat.

There are for sure some things that we do know,

Like with each year you grow and grow and grow,

And lightning bugs at dusk somehow do glow.

Or things to do, like brush your teeth at night,

And making sure to stop for a red light;

To know these things is handy and quite right.

But though THIS space seems hidden, it's quite near

That's in a place both close and far from here.

And once you've found it, then you'll really know

This secret space goes with you where you go.

And what felt scary, strange, and oh so new,

Will now seem normal as the color blue.

And everything sure from the Land of the Known

That you studied and learned and were thoroughly shown

Transforms to a place of awe and surprise

'Cause you never can know what on earth will arise.

Who knows? It could be a plate of french fries!

To help you get to this magical place,

Here's some advice that you can embrace.

Send love to all creatures both near and far

So that your heart will then glow like a star.

If anything makes you angry or mad

And you find you're exceptionally sad,

Send love to those feelings bringing you down

And love to whomever is making you frown.

Soon all the things that you have learned to name

Will shift and change and never be the same.

The roots and trunk and branches of a tree

Become a brilliant, dancing light of glee.

The sky becomes a painter's palette bold,

With blue, green, pomegranate, and some gold.

And everything sure from the Land of the Known

That you studied and learned and were thoroughly shown

Transforms to a place of awe and surprise

'Cause you never can know what on earth will arise.

Who knows? It could be a barn owl so wise!

And as this space grows stronger within you,

You'll notice changes in your point of view.

Like differences that you thought were there

Will seem to disappear into thin air.

The blooming flowers and your neighbor's cat

Will now seem linked to the naked mole rat!

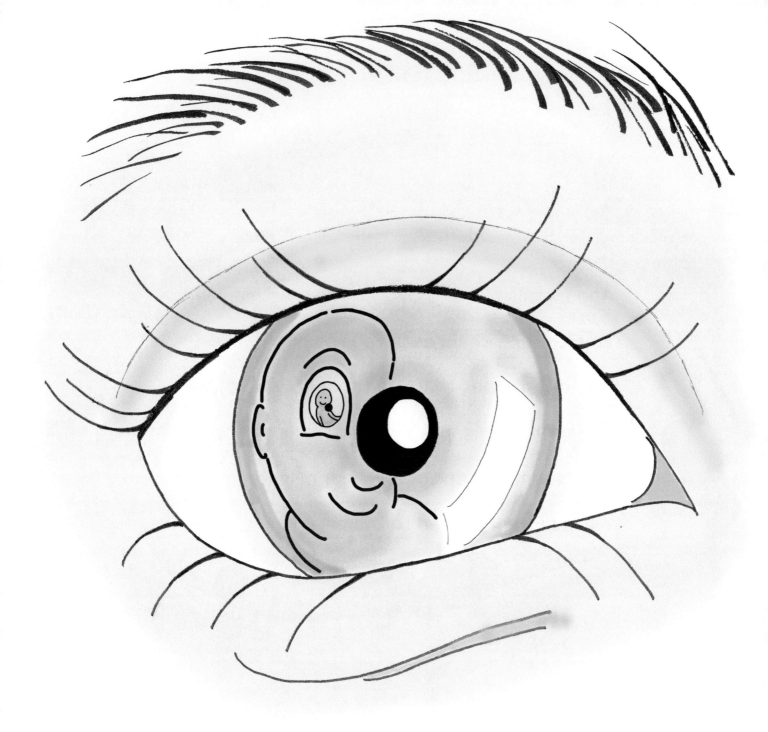

Then you may find you feel a little strange

As who you are begins to shift and change.

For as you look into another's eyes,

You see family of every shape and size.

And in the spark of their eyes, you can see

Your double staring back at you and me.

And everything sure from the Land of the Known

That you studied and learned and were thoroughly shown

Transforms to a place of awe and surprise

'Cause you never can know what on earth will arise.

Who knows? It could be a pile of bow ties!

Now this one person that you think you are

Is joining with all things near and far.

This may leave you befuddled and confused,

But if you don't get mad and blow a fuse,

A precious lesson can come from this space.

Not knowing is a magic, wondrous place.

As you are learning that we all are one,

True kindness seems to be correct and fun.

For things that are unpleasant, harsh, or mean

Just don't belong in this magical scene.

To be nasty and cruel will just feel weird,

Like if a goldfish grew a big, thick beard.

And everything sure from the Land of the Known

That you studied and learned and were thoroughly shown

Transforms to a place of awe and surprise

'Cause you never can know what on earth will arise.

Who knows? It could be Santa Clause in disguise!

The limits once put on what you could be

No longer now apply to you or me.

A dancer, lawyer, or a president,

An actor with a funny, thick accent,

Or a musician playing on their drum -

All that and much more you can now become.

If called polite or funny, mean or fat,

It will feel strange to be labeled like that.

'Cause now it's becoming quite clear to you

You're one with all, even a kangaroo!

And if someone says they know who you are,

You'll feel like you've just been stuffed in a jar.

And everything sure from the Land of the Known

That you studied and learned and were thoroughly shown

Transforms to a place of awe and surprise

'Cause you never can know what on earth will arise.

Who knows? It could be lots and lots of
blue and green striped socks with pink polka dots!

So, if you're called by anything at all,

You'll know you're more than that and not so small.

So thank them with good grace and lots of style,

While in your heart you hold a wink and a smile.

For as this space has been growing in you,

You know for sure that this one thing is true...


Though all different parts of you may be showing

You're a being that holds "The Space of Not Knowing."

Printed in the United States
by Baker & Taylor Publisher Services